I

BECOMING AN
AI AUTHOR

The Beginner's Guide to Writing and Publication of AI Assisted Books

BY JAMES T. BRADY

JAMES BRADY

Cover design by Leraynne S.

First Edition: June 2023

CONTENTS

CHAPTER 1

INTRODUCTION

As we find ourselves navigating the complex intricacies of the 21st century, one fact stands out unambiguously: we live in a rapidly evolving digital world. In every sphere, technology has ingrained itself into the fabric of our existence, revolutionizing how we work, communicate, interact, and create. One specific area of innovation, which is simultaneously fascinating and promising, lies in the intersection of technology and creativity - the application of artificial intelligence (AI) in writing. This book, an amalgamation of technological understanding and creative exploration, serves as a comprehensive guide on how to harness AI to write a book.

Before we embark on this journey into the labyrinthine world of AI and its applications in writing, it is pivotal to set out a clear understanding of what this book aims to accomplish and who it seeks to reach. Designed to be a multifaceted resource, this guide will be beneficial to a broad spectrum of readers. Whether you are an established author or an aspiring writer just starting to sketch your creative blueprint, this book will unveil new horizons in your writing process. If you are an educator aiming to blend technology into your curricula, or even a tech enthusiast eager to dive into the depths of AI-driven creativity, this guide will serve as your comprehensive roadmap. Essentially, this book is for anyone who is intrigued by the increasingly influential role of AI in content creation and wishes to understand and exploit this powerful tool.

Understanding the Power of AI

The term "artificial intelligence" has long occupied the collective human imagination. In our minds, it often paints a picture of futuristic landscapes populated by humanoid robots or, perhaps, evokes anxiety-ridden images of super-intelligent machines posing threats to humanity. Such representations, although popular in media and fiction, tend to overshadow the pragmatic and more immediate applications of AI that already permeate our lives. Stripped of its fantastical elements, AI, in its essence, is a set of algorithms and technological constructs designed to mimic and perform tasks that traditionally require human intelligence.

These tasks encompass a wide range of capabilities, such as interpreting natural language, recognizing patterns, making predictions, solving complex problems, and, most importantly for our exploration, learning from experiences to improve performance over time. Today, AI is not a distant dream but a reality, already playing a pivotal role in areas as diverse as healthcare, finance, education, and creative arts.

In the realm of writing, AI opens a treasure trove of possibilities. It has the potential to revolutionize not only how we generate and structure content, but also how we conceive of creativity itself. AI can aid in generating novel ideas, crafting, and refining content, creating compelling narratives, and even emulating human-like storytelling abilities. However, it is essential to reiterate that AI in writing is not about replacing human writers, but about augmenting human creativity. The power of AI lies in its capacity to be a tool, a digital companion that enhances our capabilities, liberates us from mundane tasks, and offers new avenues for creative expression.

This book aims to demystify the role and capabilities of AI in writing. It will equip you with the knowledge and practical skills needed to navigate the AI writing landscape, and more importantly, to harness the power of AI to transform your writing process.

Identifying the Scope of the Book

The convergence of AI and writing represents an expansive and intricate landscape. Given its vastness, it is crucial to outline the specific areas that this book will focus on. At its core, this guide serves as a hands-on manual, escorting you through the entire process of writing a book with the assistance of AI.

Our exploration will commence with an introduction to the basics of AI, with a particular emphasis on language models. Language models are a key subset of AI technology that underpins AI writing tools. These models form an essential foundation for our exploration as they unlock the ability for machines to understand, interpret, and generate human language.

As we progress, we will explore the spectrum of AI writing tools available, taking a deep dive into how they function, their capabilities, limitations, and the unique features that distinguish them from one another. This guide will lead you through the process of setting up your AI writing environment, from choosing the right tool to familiarize yourself with its interface and operations.

In the subsequent sections, we will delve into the application of AI in various stages of the writing process. Starting with how AI can be leveraged to help outline your book, we'll discuss its potential for character and plot development, and the generation of creative scenarios. Each step of the way, we'll examine how to direct your AI effectively, how to interpret its output, and how to refine and adapt its suggestions to fit your unique creative vision.

Finally, as we near the culmination of your writing process, we will explore the role of AI in editing, polishing, and refining your book. From grammar and style checks to enhancing narrative flow and continuity, AI can prove to be an invaluable ally. The guide will provide practical tips on reviewing and revising AI suggestions, ensuring your book not only aligns with your artistic intent but also meets high linguistic and stylistic standards.

It is important to note that our exploration does not stop at the completion of the writing process. The book also delves into broader topics of critical relevance in this digital age. It covers ethical considerations when using AI in writing, including concerns about originality, copyright issues, and the moral implications of AI authorship. Furthermore, it will offer insights into the promising and exciting future of AI in writing, discussing emerging trends and potential advances that are on the horizon.

Who Should Read This Book

With a comprehensive and practical approach at its heart, this book aims to cater to a wide readership. If you identify as a writer, this book will hold valuable insights, irrespective of the stage of your writing journey. You could be an experienced author with several published works, an aspiring writer taking your initial steps into the world of storytelling, or someone who writes purely for personal joy and fulfillment. This book can provide a fresh perspective, innovative techniques, and a new set of tools to augment your craft.

Educators who seek to innovate their pedagogical techniques will find this book especially useful. In an educational setting, it can serve as a valuable resource for introducing students to the practical applications of AI in writing. Whether you're teaching a course on creative writing, expository writing, or even a class on digital technology, this book provides a framework for integrating AI tools into your curriculum. By encouraging students to experiment with these tools, you can provide them with a cutting-edge skill set that combines technological proficiency with creative expression.

For tech enthusiasts and innovators, this book provides an opportunity to explore a new frontier of AI application. If you're fascinated by AI and its potential to transform various aspects of our lives, this book will serve as a comprehensive, practical, and engaging foray into the world of AI-assisted writing.

In conclusion, as we stand at the threshold of a novel era of creative expression, the coming chapters promise to take you on an enlightening journey. They aim to demystify the intricate world of AI and its role in writing, offering you the knowledge, skills, and confidence to harness these technological advances in your creative pursuits. It is my hope that this journey will not only redefine your writing process but also inspire you with the endless possibilities that the future holds. In the words of the legendary science fiction writer Arthur C. Clarke, "Any sufficiently advanced technology is indistinguishable from magic." Welcome to the future of writing, where the magic of advanced technology and the timeless beauty of human creativity blend into a new paradigm of storytelling.

The intersection of technology and writing isn't a fading trend or a mere curiosity; it is a nexus point that heralds the future of creative expression. As you navigate through this guide, you will learn that AI doesn't detract from the human element of writing but rather illuminates and enhances it. By offering new perspectives, challenging traditional concepts, and encouraging innovation, AI becomes an extension of the writer's mind - a tool as crucial to the modern writer as the pen was to Shakespeare or the typewriter was to Mark Twain.

The Era of AI in Writing

Artificial Intelligence in writing is not a prophecy for the distant future. It is the reality of the present, a revolution that's already underway. Across the globe, AI is transforming writing and content creation in numerous domains. It helps journalists cover news stories more quickly, aids marketers in crafting personalized content, assists researchers in summarizing lengthy documents, and supports authors in conjuring up intricate fictional universes.

In this era of AI-assisted writing, we're not just passive observers but active participants. We are pioneers on the cusp of a new frontier, equipped with the tools to shape the future of this landscape. The coming chapters will equip you with a map and compass, guiding you through this uncharted territory, where the powerful algorithms of AI meet the nuanced artistry of writing.

The Journey Ahead

Throughout this journey, you'll be invited to explore, experiment, and most importantly, to create. You will witness firsthand how AI can generate a range of ideas, offer unique insights, and help you overcome common challenges like writer's block. You'll experience the thrill of seeing your characters come to life and your plotlines evolve in ways you never imagined, all with the assistance of AI.

You'll also learn that AI, like any tool, isn't perfect. It has its limitations and pitfalls. It requires guidance and oversight. But these challenges don't diminish the power of AI; instead, they highlight the importance of the human touch in the creative process. This blend of human creativity and AI-assisted writing is where the true power lies, and you're about to unlock it.

Final Thoughts

In the words of novelist Terry Pratchett, "Writing is the most fun you can have by yourself." This book aims to add a new dimension to that fun, one where you're not entirely alone, but accompanied by a digital partner. This guide will equip you with the knowledge, skills, and confidence to leverage AI in your writing endeavors. Whether you're an aspiring author dreaming of publishing your first book, an educator seeking innovative teaching methods, or a tech enthusiast exploring the applications of AI, this book is your gateway to a whole new world of AI-assisted writing.

The journey of a thousand miles begins with a single step. So, let's take that step together into the future of writing, where creativity is augmented by artificial intelligence, where the stories of tomorrow are waiting to be written, and where you, the writer, stand at the helm, steering your narrative into uncharted waters. Welcome to the revolution, where human creativity meets artificial intelligence, and the magic of storytelling ascends to new heights. Welcome to the future of writing!

CHAPTER 2

UNDERSTANDING THE BASICS OF WRITING

Importance of Writing Skills

The ability to write effectively is a core skill that impacts numerous aspects of our lives. The written word serves as a primary channel of communication and expression. It transcends geographical barriers, enables the sharing of ideas, thoughts, and stories, and creates a lasting record of human experiences, knowledge, and creativity.

Mastering writing skills is not just about learning to construct grammatically correct sentences. It encompasses the art of crafting compelling narratives, creating engaging characters, and conveying emotions and ideas effectively. Writing skills can shape your ability to inform, persuade, entertain, and inspire your audience. Whether you are writing a book, a research paper, a business proposal, or a personal journal, effective writing can enhance your message's clarity, impact, and resonance.

Basics of Storytelling

At its core, storytelling is about sharing a narrative with an audience. It is an ancient art form, one that has played a critical role in human societies, cultures, and individual lives. From cave paintings to epic poems, from Shakespearean plays to modern novels, storytelling is an integral part of our shared human experience.

In its most basic form, a story comprises three essential elements: characters, setting, and plot.

1. Characters: Characters are the heart of any story. They are the individuals whose experiences the audience experiences the narrative. Characters can be complex, with their own personalities, desires, fears, strengths, and weaknesses. They can grow, change, and learn over the course of the story, which is often referred to as a character arc.

2. Setting: The setting of a story is the time and place where it occurs. This can be as broad as a country in a certain epoch or as narrow as a single room in a particular moment. The setting creates the backdrop against which the characters and their actions unfold. It can significantly influence the story's atmosphere, mood, and events.

3. Plot: The plot is the sequence of events that make up the story. It usually follows a structure that includes an introduction, rising action, climax, falling action, and conclusion. This is often referred to as the narrative arc. A well-crafted plot captivates the audience's attention, creates tension and suspense, and provides a satisfying resolution.

These elements are the building blocks of a story. However, the art of storytelling involves more than just assembling these blocks. It requires creativity, originality, and a deep understanding of human emotions, motivations, and conflicts. It involves painting vivid pictures with words, evoking emotions, and taking the reader on a memorable journey.

Exploring Various Genres

Just as a painter uses different styles and palettes to create unique pieces of art, a writer can explore various genres to tell diverse stories. Each genre has its own conventions, themes, and storytelling techniques, offering a unique lens through which to view and understand the world. Here's a brief overview of some popular genres:

1. Fiction: This genre encompasses stories that are created from the writer's imagination. Sub-genres include fantasy, science fiction, mystery, romance, horror, and historical fiction, among others. Each of these sub-genres has its own conventions and tropes, which can be both followed and subverted to create unique narratives.

2. Non-Fiction: This genre includes factual narratives such as biographies, memoirs, essays, and travelogues. Despite being based on reality, non-fiction writing also involves storytelling techniques to engage the reader and convey the author's perspective.

3. Poetry: This genre uses rhythm, rhyme, and metaphor to convey emotions, ideas, and experiences. From sonnets and haikus to free verse and spoken word, poetry offers a wide range of forms and styles to explore.

4. Drama: This genre is designed to be performed in front of an audience. It includes plays, screenplays, and radio dramas. In this genre, the emphasis is often on dialogue and stage direction.

Exploring various genres can enhance your versatility as a writer. It can broaden your narrative toolbox, introduce you to different storytelling techniques, and enrich your understanding of the myriad ways in which stories can be told.

Understanding Different Writing Styles

Writing style is the unique way a writer uses language. It reflects the writer's personality, voice, and artistic vision. Understanding different writing styles can not only help you develop your own voice but also allow you to adapt your writing to different contexts, audiences, and purposes. Here are a few styles you might come across or wish to explore:

1. Expository Writing: This style aims to inform or explain. It is fact-based, clear, and straightforward. Expository writing avoids personal bias and focuses on providing information using evidence and examples. Academic essays, news articles, and instructional manuals often use this style.

2. Descriptive Writing: This style aims to paint a picture with words. It uses detailed descriptions to evoke sensory experiences and create vivid images in the reader's mind. Descriptive writing is common in fiction, poetry, and creative non-fiction.

3. Narrative Writing: This style tells a story. It involves characters, a setting, and a plot, and it often uses techniques like dialogue, pacing, and suspense to engage the reader. Novels, short stories, and memoirs often use this style.

4. Persuasive Writing: This style aims to convince the reader of a certain viewpoint. It uses argumentation, evidence, and rhetorical techniques to persuade the reader. Opinion essays, sales pitches, and political speeches often use this style.

Each writing style serves a different purpose and requires a distinct skill set. As you hone your writing skills, you will learn to switch between these styles depending on your writing goals. Moreover, you'll develop your unique writing style that reflects your voice, your perspectives, and your creative vision.

In conclusion, writing is a versatile and powerful form of expression. It offers endless possibilities for creativity, communication, and connection. Understanding the basics of writing can provide a solid foundation for your writing journey. Whether you are an aspiring author dreaming of publishing your first book, a student striving for academic excellence, a professional seeking to communicate effectively, or a hobbyist looking to express your thoughts and emotions, mastering the art of writing can open doors to a world of opportunities.

The Writer's Toolkit

As we delve deeper into the art and craft of writing, it's important to remember that writing isn't just about inspiration —it's also about technique. Every writer has their toolkit, an assortment of skills and strategies they draw upon to bring their stories to life. Here are some of the fundamental tools you should have in your writing arsenal:

1. Grammar and Syntax: These are the rules that govern language. A solid grasp of grammar and syntax is crucial to ensure that your writing is clear, accurate, and professional. This includes understanding sentence structure, punctuation, verb tenses, and word usage, among other elements.

2. Vocabulary: A rich vocabulary allows you to express your thoughts and ideas with precision and nuance. It enables you to paint vivid pictures, convey complex emotions, and create engaging narratives. Reading widely and regularly can help enrich your vocabulary.

3. Figurative Language: Figurative language involves using words or phrases in a non-literal way to create a particular effect. This includes metaphors, similes, personification, and symbolism, among others. Figurative language can add depth, creativity, and emotional intensity to your writing.

4. Dialogue: Dialogue is a conversation between characters. Writing convincing dialogue can bring your characters to life, advance your plot, and reveal important information. Effective dialogue often involves balancing what is said with what is left unsaid.

5. Point of View: Point of view refers to who is telling the story. It could be a character in the story (first person), an external observer (third person), or even an all-knowing narrator who knows all the character's thoughts and feelings (omniscient). The choice of point of view can profoundly affect how the story is perceived and understood.

6. Show, Don't Tell: This is a classic piece of writing advice. It means using vivid descriptions, actions, and dialogue to show what's happening in the story, instead of simply telling the reader. This technique can make your writing more engaging and immersive.

The Writing Process

The writing process isn't a linear path—it's more like a journey of exploration and discovery. It typically involves several stages, including prewriting, drafting, revising, editing, and publishing. Here's a brief overview of each stage:

1. Prewriting: This is the brainstorming phase. It involves generating ideas, doing research, and planning your writing. This might involve outlining your plot, developing your characters, or exploring your themes.

2. Drafting: This is where you write your first draft. The goal of this stage isn't to create a perfect piece of writing—it's to get your ideas down on paper. Don't worry about mistakes or inconsistencies at this stage; just focus on telling your story.

3. Revising: In this stage, you take a step back and look at your work as a whole. You consider the big picture: the structure of your narrative, the development of your characters, the flow of your ideas. This is where you make major changes, like rewriting sections, rearranging paragraphs, or changing plot elements.

4. Editing: This is where you refine your work. You focus on the details: grammar, punctuation, word choice, sentence structure. This stage might involve multiple rounds of editing to ensure that your writing is as clear, accurate, and polished as possible.

5. Publishing: This is where you share your work with others. This could involve submitting your manuscript to publishers, self-publishing your book, posting your work online, or presenting it in a writing class or workshop.

Writing is a skill, a craft, and an art. It requires practice, patience, and perseverance. It requires using your imagination, expressing your thoughts clearly, and connecting with your readers. By understanding the basics of writing and honing your writing skills, you can unlock your creative potential, tell captivating stories, and make a meaningful impact through your words.

Embracing the Writing Journey

The path to becoming a proficient writer is a journey, not a destination. Along this journey, you'll encounter challenges, make discoveries, experience breakthroughs, and sometimes face setbacks. Embrace the process—the victories and the struggles alike—as every step contributes to your growth and development as a writer.

Writing is an act of courage. It involves sharing a part of yourself—your ideas, your perspectives, your emotions—with the world. It involves being open to criticism, rejection, and sometimes, misunderstanding. But it also offers the opportunity for self-expression, for touching the lives of others, for leaving a legacy through your words.

Ultimately, the beauty of writing lies not just in the finished product but in the process—the act of bringing your ideas to life, the joy of seeing your characters evolve, the thrill of weaving your narrative. It's about the journey, the learning, the personal growth, and the connection you make with your readers. So, as you embark on your writing journey, remember to embrace each moment, each challenge, and each success, for every word you write contributes to your unique writer's journey.

As we close this chapter, remember that writing is a craft that can be learned, honed, and mastered. It requires commitment, patience, and perseverance. With the right tools, knowledge, and a passion for storytelling, you are well-equipped to embark on your writing journey. Whether your dream is to write a best-selling novel, a thought-provoking essay, a compelling screenplay, or a heartfelt poem, understanding the basics of writing is the first step towards turning that dream into reality.

In the next chapter, we will delve into the fascinating world of AI and explore how it can serve as a powerful tool in your writer's toolkit. Just as a skilled carpenter uses a variety of tools to build a beautiful piece of furniture, a skilled writer can use AI to craft a captivating narrative. So, join us as we step into the future of writing—a future where human creativity meets artificial intelligence, where the stories of tomorrow are waiting to be written, and where you, the writer, stand at the helm, steering your narrative into uncharted waters.

CHAPTER 3

DEMYSTIFYING AI

Defining Artificial Intelligence (AI)

Artificial Intelligence (AI) is a multifaceted field of computer science that involves creating machines capable of simulating human intelligence. It encompasses a wide range of subfields, from machine learning and natural language processing to robotics and computer vision. AI is fundamentally about creating algorithms that enable machines to learn from experience, adapt to new inputs, and perform tasks that usually require human intelligence.

AI is rooted in the concept of creating intelligent agents — entities that perceive their environment and make decisions to maximize their chances of achieving their goals. These intelligent agents can be as simple as a chess-playing computer program or as complex as an autonomous driving system. The underlying principle, however, remains the same: AI involves creating systems that can perceive, reason, learn, and act in ways that exhibit human-like intelligence.

Brief History of AI in Writing

The application of AI in writing is a relatively recent development, but it has roots that trace back to the earliest days of computer science. The dream of creating machines that could generate human-like text has been a recurring theme in science fiction and academia for decades. However, it's only in the last few years that this dream has started to become a reality.

The journey of AI in writing began with simple programs that could generate random combinations of words or mimic basic linguistic structures. In the 1960s, Joseph Weizenbaum at MIT developed a program called ELIZA that could mimic a psychotherapist by using preprogrammed responses to user inputs. Although ELIZA had no understanding of the conversation, it demonstrated the potential for machines to generate text that seemed human-like on the surface.

In the following decades, researchers continued to develop more sophisticated text generation systems, from rule-based systems that could generate specific types of text (such as weather reports or sports summaries) to statistical models that used large corpora of text to predict the probability of a word given its context.

The advent of machine learning and, more specifically, deep learning, marked a turning point in the history of AI in writing. By leveraging large amounts of data and powerful computational resources, researchers were able to train models that could generate increasingly coherent and diverse text. One of the major breakthroughs came in 2018, with the introduction of the transformer architecture by Vaswani et al., which forms the basis for many of the state-of-the-art text generation models today.

Since then, there have been rapid advancements in AI writing technology. From Google's BERT model that excels at understanding the context of words in a sentence, to OpenAI's GPT-2 and GPT-3 models that can generate impressively human-like text, AI is transforming the landscape of writing in unprecedented ways.

Different Types of AI (NLP, GPT-x, etc.)

AI encompasses a broad spectrum of technologies, each with its strengths and applications. When it comes to AI in writing, two types of AI are particularly relevant: Natural Language Processing (NLP) and Generative Pretrained Transformers (GPT).

1. Natural Language Processing (NLP): NLP is a subfield of AI that focuses on the interaction between computers and human language. It involves teaching machines to understand, interpret, generate, and manipulate human language. NLP encompasses various tasks, from speech recognition and sentiment analysis to machine translation and text summarization. The goal of NLP is to enable computers to understand and respond to human language in a way that is both meaningful and useful.

2. Generative Pretrained Transformers (GPT): GPT is a type of language processing AI developed by OpenAI. The 'GPT' model uses a transformer architecture, which allows it to consider the context of each word and its relationship to other words in a text. The model is pretrained on a vast corpus of text from the internet, and it learns to predict the next word in a sentence given the preceding words. This ability to generate coherent and contextually appropriate text makes GPT particularly effective for tasks like text generation, translation, and summarization.

Benefits and Limitations of AI in Writing

AI offers numerous benefits in the realm of writing. It can automate routine writing tasks, provide real-time writing assistance, generate creative ideas, and offer new ways to engage with text. Here are some ways AI can enhance the writing process:

1. Automation: AI can automate mundane writing tasks, such as drafting routine emails or generating standard reports, freeing up time for more creative and strategic tasks.

2. Writing Assistance: AI-powered writing tools can provide real-time feedback on grammar, punctuation, clarity, tone, and style, helping writers improve their writing in real time.

3. Idea Generation: AI can generate writing prompts, story ideas, or even entire drafts, providing a springboard for creativity and reducing the pressure of the blank page.

4. Personalization: AI can customize content based on individual preferences, reading levels, or learning goals, enhancing engagement and comprehension.

However, AI also has its limitations in writing. Here are a few:

1. Lack of Understanding: While AI can simulate human-like text, it doesn't truly understand the text it generates. It lacks the ability to comprehend nuanced meanings, cultural references, or complex emotions that are inherent in human language.

2. Ethical Concerns: AI writing tools can potentially be misused to generate misleading or harmful content, such as fake news or spam.

3. Overdependence: Overreliance on AI writing tools can limit a writer's own creative process and critical thinking skills. Writing is not just about generating text; it's also about expressing unique ideas, developing a personal voice, and engaging with the audience in a meaningful way.

As we delve deeper into the world of AI in writing, it's crucial to recognize both the potential and the pitfalls of this technology. AI can be a powerful tool in a writer's toolkit, but it's not a replacement for human creativity, judgment, and empathy. The key is to use AI as a tool to augment our abilities, not to overshadow them.

In the coming chapters, we'll explore more about how to effectively use AI in writing, how to collaborate with AI to enhance your creativity, and how to navigate the ethical implications of AI in writing. As we embark on this journey, keep in mind that AI is not an end in itself; it's a tool to help you achieve your writing goals, tell your stories, and express your unique voice in the world of words.

The Mechanics of AI in Writing

Before we can truly be comfortable using this new tool, we must dig a little deeper into the mechanics of AI when applied to writing. This exploration will enhance your understanding of how AI can augment your writing process.

AI writing tools leverage sophisticated machine learning algorithms, which learn patterns from large volumes of text data. Once these algorithms are trained, they can generate human-like text that mirrors the style and structure of the input data.

Take GPT-3, for instance. This model has been trained on diverse internet text, and its generative capabilities are staggering. It can complete sentences, write essays, answer questions, and even create poetry. However, the crucial thing to remember is that GPT-3 and similar models generate text based on patterns they've learned. They don't understand the text in the same way humans do.

Despite this, AI can be a powerful tool for writers. If you're struggling with writer's block, for example, AI can provide inspiration by generating ideas or drafting sections of text. Or if you're drafting an important email or document, AI tools can provide real-time feedback on grammar, style, and tone. AI can also help with tasks such as keyword research, SEO optimization, and content personalization.

Harnessing AI in Your Writing Process

How can you harness AI in your writing process? Here are some suggestions:

1. Brainstorming: Use AI to generate ideas or prompts when you're stuck. You can input a few key words or an initial sentence, and let the AI suggest ways to continue.

2. Drafting: Use AI to draft sections of text. You can then build on this draft, adding your own insights, personality, and creativity.

3. Editing: Use AI for real-time writing feedback. AI can point out grammar errors, suggest improvements in style and clarity, and even help optimize your text for SEO.

4. Learning: Use AI to learn from your favorite writers. Some AI tools can analyze the style of specific authors, helping you understand their writing techniques and apply them to your own work.

5. Engaging: Use AI to personalize your content for different audiences, enhancing engagement and impact. AI can help you tailor your language, tone, and content to match your audience's preferences and needs.

Future Perspectives of AI in Writing

AI is set to transform the writing landscape in profound ways. As AI technology continues to advance, we can expect more sophisticated writing tools that offer greater customization, real-time feedback, and creative possibilities.

However, as we embrace the potential of AI, we must also grapple with its ethical and societal implications. As writers, we have a responsibility to use AI in a way that respects privacy, promotes truth, and fosters positive engagement. We must also strive to maintain a healthy balance between AI assistance and our own creative agency.

AI can be a powerful tool for writers, but it doesn't replace the need for human creativity, insight, and empathy. In fact, these human qualities have become even more important in an AI-driven world. As we navigate this new landscape, let's remember to use AI not as a crutch, but as a tool that empowers us to write with greater creativity, clarity, and impact.

I hope you have begun to realize that AI is not just changing the way we write, it's expanding our notion of what is possible in writing. As we embark on this journey of exploration and discovery, let's embrace the potential of AI, while also respecting its limitations. Let's remember that at the heart of every great piece of writing is a human story, a human voice, a human connection — elements that AI can augment, but never replace. In the end, it's not about AI versus human; it's about AI and human, working together to create a richer, more vibrant world of words.

How AI Learns Language

Deepening our understanding of AI in writing necessitates an examination of how AI learns language. As mentioned earlier, AI, such as the GPT models, learns language patterns from a large dataset comprised of diverse text from the internet. But how exactly does this happen?

The process begins with training the AI on a massive volume of text, allowing the model to observe and learn patterns in human language. The AI sees countless examples of sentences, phrases, paragraphs, and even whole essays, and through this exposure, it starts to recognize patterns. It's important to note that this isn't understanding in the human sense; rather, the AI is noticing statistical regularities in the data it has been trained on.

For example, the AI learns that the word "sky" is often followed by words like "blue," "cloudy," or "stars." Over time, and with enough data, the AI starts to generate sentences that follow the grammatical and stylistic norms it has observed in its training data. But the AI doesn't understand the meaning of these sentences. It doesn't know what a "blue sky" looks like or what "stars" are. It is merely following patterns it has seen during its training.

This training process highlights both the strengths and weaknesses of AI in writing. On one hand, it can generate text that is remarkably human-like, given that it has been trained on human-generated text. On the other hand, the text generated by AI lacks the depth of understanding, the nuance, and the context that human writers bring to their work.

Human Creativity and AI

As AI continues to evolve and improve, it's easy to wonder about the role of human creativity in the writing process. Can AI replace the creative insights, the empathetic understanding, and the nuanced storytelling of human writers?

While AI can mimic human-like text generation, it cannot replicate the complexity of human creativity. Creativity involves more than just generating text that follows grammatical and stylistic norms. It involves crafting narratives that resonate with human experiences, evoking emotions that stir the human heart, and expressing insights that enlighten the human mind. It involves understanding not just the words, but the world they represent, and the myriad of human experiences that the world encompasses.

AI can generate a poem that follows the stylistic norms of poetry, but it can't appreciate the beauty of a sunset, the poignancy of a farewell, or the joy of a reunion. It can't understand the complex interplay of emotions, thoughts, and experiences that give rise to the human condition. Therefore, while AI can be a valuable tool for generating text, it can't replace the creative essence that makes writing a fundamentally human endeavor.

As we move forward in the age of AI, it's crucial that we celebrate and cultivate our human creativity. We can leverage AI as a tool to enhance our writing process, but we must remember that the heart of writing lies in our ability to tell stories, to connect with others, and to express our unique perspective on the world. AI can assist us in this endeavor, but it cannot replace us.

Summary

As we close this chapter on demystifying AI, let's remember that AI is a tool, a means to an end, and not an end in itself. It's a powerful technology that can transform the way we write, but it doesn't negate the need for human creativity, empathy, and understanding. It can improve our writing process, but it can't replace the unique insights and experiences we bring to our work.

As writers, we stand on the cusp of a new era—an era where we can harness the power of AI to tell our stories, express our ideas, and connect with our readers in new and exciting ways. But as we embrace this potential, let's also remember to honor and cultivate the human heart of writing, for it is this heart that makes our stories truly resonate.

Let's look forward to exploring how we can integrate AI into our writing process in the next chapter, where we will dive into practical applications and methods to co-create with AI, making the best use of this incredible tool while preserving the integrity of our human voice and creative expression. We'll also explore the potential pitfalls and ethical considerations when writing with AI. So, stay tuned, keep exploring, and keep writing, for there is much to discover on this exciting journey.

CHAPTER 4

A PRIMER ON LANGUAGE MODELS

Understanding Natural Language Processing (NLP)

Natural Language Processing (NLP) is a subfield of artificial intelligence that focuses on the interaction between computers and humans through language. It allows computers to understand, interpret, generate, and make sense of human language in a valuable and meaningful way. NLP involves several complex and interrelated tasks, such as speech recognition, natural language understanding, natural language generation, and machine translation.

NLP has several real-world applications, including but not limited to, search engines, voice assistants like Siri and Alexa, language translation apps, and, of course, AI writing tools. These applications utilize NLP to understand and generate human language, making our interactions with computers more natural and intuitive.

The core challenge of NLP lies in the complexity and ambiguity of human language. Natural language is rich, expressive, and filled with nuance. It's characterized by ambiguity, idiosyncrasy, and a high degree of variability. Therefore, enabling computers to understand and generate human language is no small feat. It requires sophisticated algorithms, vast amounts of data, and significant computational power.

What are Language Models?

A language model is a type of artificial intelligence model that understands, generates, and works with human language. These models are trained on large amounts of text data and learn to predict the probability of a sequence of words. In simpler terms, given a certain number of words, a language model can predict the next word or words that are most likely to come next.

Language models have been around for some time, but recent advancements in machine learning and AI have led to the development of more powerful and sophisticated models. These newer models, like the Transformer-based models, can understand context, preserving long-term dependencies in text, and generating human-like text.

How do Language Models Work?

Language models learn to predict text based on the statistical patterns they observe in the data they are trained on. During the training process, these models see numerous examples of sentences and phrases. Through these examples, they learn the probability of a word given the preceding words.

Take the sentence "The cat sat on the ___," for instance. A language model trained on English text will predict that the next word is likely to be "mat" because, in its training data, it has frequently seen the word "mat" follow the phrase "The cat sat on the."

However, it's crucial to remember that these models don't understand language or text in the same way humans do. They don't understand meaning, context, or nuance to the same degree. Their predictions are based purely on patterns they have seen in their training data.

Popular Language Models and Their Applications in Writing

There are several popular language models that have significantly impacted the field of AI writing. Let's explore a few:

1. GPT-3: Developed by OpenAI, GPT-3 (Generative Pretrained Transformer 3) is one of the most powerful language models to date. With 175 billion machine learning parameters, GPT-3 can generate incredibly human-like text. It can answer questions, write essays, summarize text, translate languages, and even create poetry. It's being used in various applications, from drafting emails to generating code to creating written content.

2. BERT: BERT (Bidirectional Encoder Representations from Transformers) is a Transformer-based model developed by Google. Unlike previous models, BERT is designed to understand the context of words in a sentence by looking at the words that come before and after it. This bidirectional understanding makes BERT particularly effective for tasks like question answering, language translation, and text summarization.

3. RoBERTa: RoBERTa is a variant of BERT, developed by Facebook AI. It follows the same fundamental design as BERT but includes several tweaks in the training process that improve the model's performance and efficiency.

4. T5: T5 (Text-to-Text Transfer Transformer) is a model developed by Google that takes a unique approach to NLP tasks. It treats every NLP task as a text-to-text translation problem. For instance, a question-answering task is seen as translating a question into an answer. This unified framework allows T5 to handle a wide range of NLP tasks.

5. XLNet: XLNet is another variant of the Transformer model, which overcomes some of the limitations of BERT. Unlike

BERT, which predicts words independently, XLNet considers the probability of a word given all the other words in the sentence, not just the words before it.

These models, and others like them, have wide-ranging applications in writing. They can generate text, provide writing suggestions, answer questions, summarize long articles, and more. They can be used as standalone writing tools or integrated into larger platforms to augment the writing process.

For instance, GPT-3 can help generate creative story ideas, write compelling product descriptions, or draft insightful articles. BERT can assist in understanding and answering complex questions, making it valuable for writing research papers or technical documents. T5 can handle multiple NLP tasks, making it a versatile tool for any writing task.

The Mechanics of AI Language Models

Language models' functionality might seem almost magical, but the principles underlying their operation are purely mathematical, based on a branch of AI called machine learning. Machine learning models, including language models, learn from data without being explicitly programmed to perform a specific task. Instead, they identify patterns in data and make predictions based on these patterns.

In the context of language models, the learning process starts by feeding the model a massive amount of text, which could include books, websites, and other forms of written content. The model is then tasked with predicting the next word in a sentence given all the previous words. Through this repetitive process, the model learns the statistical structure of the language.

For instance, after seeing the sentence "The sky is blue" numerous times in different contexts, the model learns that the word "blue" often follows "The sky is". This process takes place on a much larger scale and involves complex mathematical operations.

Advanced language models like GPT-3, BERT, and others go beyond simple word prediction, though. They understand the context of sentences, recognize the meaning of words based on surrounding text, and can generate detailed, coherent paragraphs of text.

Exploring the Inner Workings of AI Language Models

As we dig deeper into the inner workings of AI language models, it's crucial to understand that they operate based on a concept known as machine learning, specifically a type called deep learning. Deep learning is a subfield of machine learning inspired by the structure and function of the human brain, specifically a concept known as neural networks.

In deep learning, artificial neural networks with various layers - hence, the 'deep' in the name - are built. These layers are essentially algorithms or mathematical models each performing a specific task. The input data is processed through these layers, transformed along the way, until the final layer outputs the result.

In the case of AI language models, the architecture of choice is a variant of these neural networks called transformer models, which are particularly suited to handling sequential data, such as text. Transformer models leverage a mechanism called 'attention' that allows them to weigh the impact of different words when generating predictions.

For example, in the sentence, "John, who lived in Paris for ten years and loves art, went to the museum," the model understands that 'John' and 'went to the museum' are more closely related than 'lived in Paris for ten years' and 'loves art'. This understanding of context allows the model to generate human-like text that maintains subject consistency and coherency.

Fine-Tuning AI Language Models

It's also important to understand that while large pre-trained models like GPT-3 are powerful, they may not always generate text that aligns with a specific writing style or domain. This is where the concept of fine-tuning comes in.

Fine-tuning is a process where the pre-trained language model is further trained on a smaller, specific dataset. For example, if you're writing a book about astronomy and you want the AI to generate content that aligns with this topic, you might fine-tune the model on a corpus of astronomy books.

Fine-tuning adjusts the weights of the model - the parameters that the model learned during its initial training - to better align with the new, specific data. Post fine-tuning, the model becomes more adept at generating text that aligns with the style and substance of the specific corpus it was fine-tuned on.

Controlling AI Language Models

Another crucial aspect of working with AI language models is understanding how to control their output. Despite the leaps in performance and sophistication, AI language models are fundamentally prediction machines, and their outputs are subject to the input they are provided.

When feeding the model, a well-crafted prompt is often key to getting useful output. For example, if you're using GPT-3 to generate a blog post about the latest developments in AI, the prompt could be as detailed as the first paragraph of the blog post, outlining what the post will cover. The more specific and structured the prompt, the more likely the model is to generate meaningful and coherent output.

Apart from the prompt, other factors can be tweaked to control the model's output. These can include the 'temperature' parameter, which controls the randomness of the model's output. A lower temperature makes the output more deterministic, while a higher temperature encourages more randomness.

In conclusion, understanding the underlying mechanics of AI language models, from their training to fine-tuning, to the ways to control their output, is essential as we seek to harness their potential for writing. While they are complex systems, a fundamental understanding of their workings allows us to work with them effectively, leading to outputs that can assist and enhance our writing process.

Ethics and AI Writing

Although we will cover the topic more in-depth in a later chapter it is important to briefly discuss ethics in any overview of AI Language Models. As we harness the power of AI in writing, it's crucial to consider ethical implications. For instance, the potential for AI to generate misinformation or 'deepfake' text is a concern. Ensuring that AI-generated content is transparently labelled and used responsibly is paramount.

Moreover, AI models can unintentionally perpetuate biases present in their training data. It's essential to be aware of these potential biases and work towards developing fair and equitable AI systems.

AI language models have truly opened up exciting new possibilities in writing, offering tools that can augment our creativity, efficiency, and productivity. However, as we leverage these tools, it's crucial to navigate their capabilities, limitations, and ethical implications with care and consideration.

CHAPTER 5

WRITING WITH AI: WHERE TO START

Choosing the Right AI Writing Tool

Before you begin writing with AI, it's crucial to select an AI writing tool that fits your needs. There are several factors to consider when making this decision, including the tool's capabilities, ease of use, cost, and the support and resources available.

1. Capabilities: Different AI writing tools offer different capabilities. Some tools, like OpenAI's GPT-3, offer robust language generation capabilities, capable of generating everything from emails to blog posts to poetry. Other tools might focus on specific writing tasks, like drafting business reports, creating advertising copy, or writing code. Identify your writing needs and choose a tool that can address them effectively.

2. Ease of Use: Writing with AI should streamline your writing process, not complicate it. Choose a tool that is user-friendly and intuitive. A steep learning curve can slow you down and diminish the benefits of using AI for writing.

3. Cost: The cost of AI writing tools varies widely. Some tools offer a free tier, while others require a monthly or yearly subscription. Some might even charge based on the amount of text generated. Factor in your budget when choosing a tool, but also consider the value the tool brings to your writing process.

4. Support and Resources: Writing with AI can be complex, especially if you're new to it. Having access to helpful resources—such as guides, tutorials, and customer support—can make your journey smoother. Check what resources and support the tool provides before making your decision.

Once you've chosen your AI writing tool, it's time to set up your AI writing environment.

Setting up Your AI Writing Environment

Setting up your AI writing environment involves a few steps, depending on the tool you've chosen. Here are the general steps you should expect:

1. Registration: Most AI writing tools require you to create an account. This process typically involves providing an email address and creating a password. Some tools might also require additional information.

2. Installation: Some AI writing tools operate entirely online, while others require you to install software on your computer. Follow the tool's instructions for installation if necessary.

3. Configuration: Once you've registered and installed the tool (if necessary), you might need to configure certain settings. This could involve setting your language preference, choosing the format of the text output, and other similar settings.

4. Training: If the AI writing tool allows for fine-tuning on specific datasets (as discussed in the previous chapter), you might need to train the AI on your specific writing style or on text relevant to your writing project.

By following these steps, you should have your AI writing environment set up. Remember, these steps can vary depending on the tool you're using, so always refer to the tool's specific guidelines.

Basic Commands and Operations

Now that you've set up your AI writing environment, it's time to start writing. Most AI writing tools use a system of commands or prompts to control the AI's output. The specifics can vary, but here are some general principles:

1. Understanding Prompts: The AI generates text based on a prompt you provide. This prompt could be a single word, a sentence, or a paragraph. The AI will use the prompt as the starting point and generate text that follows from it. For instance, if you provide the prompt "Once upon a time, in a faraway kingdom,", the AI might continue with a fairy tale-like story.

2. Using Commands: Some AI writing tools allow you to use explicit commands to direct the AI's writing. For example, you might write "Translate the following text into French:" followed by the text you want to be translated. The AI will understand the command and execute it.

3. Setting Parameters: Certain parameters can be adjusted to influence the AI's output. These parameters might include "temperature", which controls the randomness of the output, and "max tokens", which controls the length of the output. These parameters can be tweaked according to your specific needs.

4. Iterating and Refining: Writing with AI is often an iterative process. You provide a prompt, review the AI's output, refine your prompt or parameters, and repeat the process until you're satisfied with the result.

Remember, each AI writing tool has its own set of features and commands. Be sure to familiarize yourself with the tool's specific guidelines.

Writing with AI can be an exciting and fruitful endeavor. By choosing the right tool, setting up your AI writing environment, and mastering basic commands and operations, you're well on your way to unlocking new possibilities in your writing journey. As you get more comfortable with writing with AI, you'll find that it opens a world of creativity and efficiency.

Deep Dive Into AI Writing Tools

Now that we've laid down the initial groundwork, let's take a closer look at some of the popular AI writing tools in the market and what each brings to the table:

1. OpenAI's GPT-3: GPT-3, developed by OpenAI, is a state-of-the-art AI writing tool. It's a robust language model that can generate impressive human-like text. OpenAI provides an API, which allows you to integrate GPT-3's capabilities into your own applications. However, it requires some technical know-how and does not come with a user interface, making it more suitable for developers.

2. Jarvis (formerly Jarvis.ai): Jarvis is a user-friendly AI writing tool that leverages GPT-3 technology. It offers a range of features, including a long-form assistant, which can help write blog posts, scripts, and more.

3. Kuki.ai: Kuki is an AI chatbot platform that can also be used for writing. It offers customizable AI personalities and the ability to learn and remember user inputs, making it great for creating interactive stories or dialogue.

4. Outwrite: Outwrite is an AI writing assistant that helps with proofreading and editing. It checks your writing for grammar, spelling, and punctuation errors, and offers suggestions to improve style and clarity.

5. Copy.ai: Copy.ai is a platform that uses AI to create marketing copy. It offers templates for a wide range of marketing content, including social media posts, email newsletters, and website copy.

It's worth noting that some tools offer free trials or free tiers, so you can test them out and see which one works best for you before making a financial commitment.

Mastering Your AI Writing Tool

As you get started with your chosen AI writing tool, here are some tips to help you master it:

1. Start with Simple Tasks: If you're new to writing with AI, it's advisable to start with simple writing tasks to get a feel for how your tool works. This could involve writing an email, creating a to-do list, or drafting a short blog post.

2. Experiment with Different Prompts: The quality of the AI's output is largely dependent on the quality of the input prompt. Try out different prompts to see which ones yield the best results. You might find that certain phrasings or structures work better than others.

3. Use Templates If Available: Some AI writing tools offer templates for common writing tasks. These templates can serve as a great starting point and can help you get familiar with the tool's capabilities.

4. Learn from Mistakes: Not all AI-generated text will be perfect. Sometimes, the AI might misunderstand the prompt, or generate text that doesn't quite hit the mark. Use these instances as learning opportunities. Understand why the AI made a mistake and adjust your prompt or parameters accordingly.

5. Stay Involved: AI is a powerful tool, but it doesn't replace the human touch. Stay involved in the writing process, edit, and refine the AI-generated text, and make sure it aligns with your vision and voice.

By experimenting, learning from your experiences, and staying involved in the writing process, you'll be able to master your AI writing tool and get the most out of it.

Further Considerations and Best Practices

After you have mastered your chosen AI tool, there are further considerations and best practices to ensure a smooth and efficient writing process:

1. Ethical Considerations: AI writing tools, especially those that generate text, have the potential to be used unethically. For instance, generating large volumes of low-quality content for spam or misleading information can have harmful effects. It's essential to use AI responsibly and ethically. Always respect copyright laws and avoid using AI to create or spread false or misleading information.

2. Privacy and Security: When using AI writing tools, particularly cloud-based ones, your data might be stored and processed on the tool's servers. Be aware of the tool's privacy policy and data handling practices. If you're dealing with sensitive information, choose a tool with robust security measures.

3. Balance AI Aid with Human Creativity: While AI can generate text, it doesn't replace the need for human creativity and intuition. The AI is a tool, an assistant, that can help streamline your writing process, but it doesn't understand the nuances, emotions, or the unique creative elements that a human writer brings to a piece of work. Keep this balance in mind as you write with AI.

4. Continual Learning: AI writing tools, like all technology, are continually evolving. Keep up with the latest developments in the tool you're using. Participate in community forums, follow the tool's updates, and always be open to learning new features and techniques.

5. Regular Breaks and Mindfulness: Using AI tools can

sometimes mean you spend longer periods in front of a screen. Remember to take regular breaks to rest your eyes and mind. Consider integrating mindfulness techniques into your writing process to maintain focus and reduce stress.

Closing Thoughts

Writing with AI is a journey filled with exploration and learning. It opens a world of possibilities, enabling you to create content more efficiently and exploring styles or formats you may not have considered before. By understanding your AI writing tool's ins and outs and using it responsibly and creatively, you can enhance your writing process and expand your horizons.

As this chapter draws to a close, remember that the journey doesn't end here. Keep exploring, keep learning, and most importantly, keep writing.

CHAPTER 6

COLLABORATIVE WRITING WITH AI

Guiding the AI: How to Give Effective Prompts

Writing with AI is a collaborative process. You are not merely a passive user, but an active participant, guiding the AI and shaping its output. One of the most critical aspects of this collaboration is how to give effective prompts.

Prompts are essentially instructions or directions that guide the AI. Depending on the sophistication of the AI model, it can range from simple word prompts to complex instructions. The quality and clarity of your prompts can significantly impact the quality of the AI's output. Here are some tips on how to give effective prompts:

1. Be Specific: AI models, while powerful, do not possess human-like understanding or context. The more specific your prompt, the better the AI can generate the desired output. For instance, if you want the AI to write a blog post about the benefits of eating organic food, your prompt could be "Write a persuasive blog post about the five main benefits of eating organic food for health-conscious consumers."

2. Provide Context: Giving context helps the AI understand what you're asking for better. If you're writing a continuation of a story or a piece, provide some background details or a summary before giving your prompt.

3. Experiment with Different Formats: There's no one-size-fits-all format for prompts. Different tasks might require different types of prompts. You might need to experiment with several prompt formats before you find what works best for your task.

4. Adjust Your Language: AI models can typically understand and generate text in multiple languages. However, some languages or dialects might be more challenging for the AI to handle than others. If you find that the AI struggles with a certain language or dialect, you might need to adjust your language or use a more standard dialect.

Iterating and Refining AI Output

AI-generated text might not always be perfect on the first try. Often, you'll need to iterate and refine the AI's output to get it to where you want it to be. Here's how you can do that:

1. Review the AI's Output: Read through the AI's output carefully. Look for any errors, inconsistencies, or areas that need improvement. Make a note of these issues.

2. Refine Your Prompt: If the AI's output is not what you expected, your prompt might need refining. Think about how you can make your prompt clearer or more specific. Sometimes, rephrasing the prompt or providing more context can yield better results.

3. Adjust Parameters: Most AI writing tools allow you to adjust certain parameters that influence the AI's output. For example, the 'temperature' parameter controls the randomness of the output. A higher temperature results in more random output, while a lower temperature makes the output more focused and deterministic.

4. Edit the AI's Output: Don't be afraid to manually edit the AI's output. You might need to correct errors, add details, or rephrase sentences to make the text better fit your needs. Remember, AI is a tool to assist you, not replace you.

Balancing Human Creativity and AI Assistance

While AI can generate impressive human-like text, it doesn't replace the need for human creativity. It's essential to find a balance between relying on the AI for assistance and maintaining your unique human touch.

1. AI as a Tool: Treat the AI as a tool to assist you in your writing process. It can help generate ideas, draft text, and streamline your writing process. However, it doesn't understand the nuances, emotions, and personal experiences that you, as a human writer, bring to your writing.

2. Maintain Your Voice: AI models are trained on large datasets and try to mimic human-like text based on these datasets. This means that AI-generated text might sometimes lack a distinct voice or style. As a writer, it's essential to review and edit the AI's output to ensure it aligns with your unique voice and style.

3. Harness Human Creativity: AI is excellent for tasks involving patterns, consistency, and large volumes of data. However, when it comes to creativity, humans still have the upper hand. Use your creativity to come up with unique ideas, plot twists, character developments, or poetic expressions. The AI can then help you bring these ideas to life.

Collaborative writing with AI is an exciting new frontier in the world of writing. By learning how to guide the AI, iterate and refine its output, and balance human creativity with AI assistance, you can unlock new possibilities and take your writing to the next level.

Enhancing Collaboration: Working Hand-in-Hand with AI

Now that we've covered the basic aspects of collaborative writing with AI, it's time to discuss how to enhance this collaboration. The goal is to create a symbiotic relationship where the strengths of AI and human creativity are leveraged to produce compelling content.

Experimentation is Key: AI can be unpredictable. Despite giving clear instructions, there might be instances where the AI deviates or takes a different approach. Instead of getting frustrated, consider these moments as an opportunity for creativity. Perhaps the AI has provided a new perspective or angle that you hadn't considered before. Don't hesitate to experiment with the AI's suggestions, and remember, you have the final say on what to accept and what to refine.

Leveraging AI for Brainstorming: One of the areas where AI shines is in generating ideas. If you're stuck on a plot point, a blog topic, or a product description, AI can quickly generate multiple options. The trick is to use these ideas as a springboard, sparking your creativity and providing a starting point from which you can expand.

Quality Control: While AI is improving rapidly, it's not infallible. There may be instances where the AI makes factual errors, grammatical mistakes, or stylistic blunders. You need to ensure that you are vigilant in proofreading the AI's work. Luckily, AI can assist here too, with many AI-powered proofreading tools available to help catch mistakes and enhance your writing.

AI as a Learning Tool

AI can also help you grow as a writer. By analyzing the AI's suggestions and output, you can gain insights into different writing styles, sentence structures, and storytelling techniques. You can also learn from the AI's mistakes, understanding where it falls short, and focusing on those areas in your writing practice.

Collaborating with AI can, at first, feel like uncharted territory, but with time, you will understand how to guide the AI and mold its output to fit your requirements. You will learn to make the most of its strengths while filling in where it falls short with your creativity and human touch.

Setting Realistic Expectations

While AI is a powerful tool, it's crucial to set realistic expectations. AI, even with the most advanced models, is not a magic wand that will do all the work for you.

Understand the Limitations: AI models, as of the time of this book's writing don't understand the world in the way humans do. They don't understand facts, emotions, personal experiences, or the nuances of human language fully. They generate text based on patterns they've learned from their training data.

AI Doesn't Replace Human Writers: AI is a tool, a powerful one, but it does not replace human writers. The creativity, personal experiences, emotions, and unique perspective a human brings to their writing is something AI can't replicate. A piece of writing is not just a collection of words, but a reflection of the writer's thoughts, feelings, and worldview, and that is something unique to each individual.

Adapting to the AI Landscape

As we move deeper into the era of AI, it becomes crucial for writers to adapt to this changing landscape. AI is not a threat to writers but a tool that can be harnessed to unlock new avenues of creativity and productivity. Here's how you can adapt to this landscape:

Continuous Learning: AI is a rapidly evolving field. Staying updated with the latest advancements in AI technology will help you harness its full potential. Subscribe to AI newsletters, participate in AI communities, attend webinars and workshops, and always keep an open mind for learning.

Collaborating with Others: Collaborating with other writers who use AI can provide fresh perspectives and insights. You can learn from their experiences, share your own, and collectively grow. Collaboration could also extend to tech experts, AI developers, or data scientists who can provide deeper insights into the technical aspects of AI.

Adjusting to AI Quirks: Like humans, AI also has its quirks. It can sometimes generate surprising or unexpected results. Learning to adjust to these quirks can add a unique flavor to your writing process. Embrace the unexpected as a part of your creative journey.

Building Your AI Skills: As you continue to use AI for writing, you'll develop a set of unique skills. You'll learn how to communicate effectively with AI, how to guide it, and how to integrate its output into your work. These skills, though different from traditional writing skills, are valuable in the AI-augmented writing world.

Final Thoughts

Collaborative writing with AI is a partnership. It's about combining the analytical and pattern-recognition strengths of AI with the creativity, critical thinking, and emotional intelligence of a human writer. This chapter has provided insights into how you can guide AI, iterate, and refine its output, and maintain a balance between AI assistance and human creativity.

By embracing AI and learning to work with it, you can enhance your writing capabilities, reduce the burden of repetitive tasks, and focus on what you love most about writing—telling a story, sharing knowledge, expressing your thoughts and emotions, and connecting with your readers.

As we step into a future where AI plays an increasing role in writing, remember that you, as a writer, are irreplaceable. The uniqueness, the creativity, the personal touch that you bring to your writing—that's something no AI can replicate. AI is here to assist you, not replace you. So, embrace it, learn from it, and let it assist you in your writing journey.

CHAPTER 7

CRAFTING THE STRUCTURE OF YOUR BOOK WITH AI

Planning Your Book Outline with AI

Outlining is a crucial step in writing a book. It gives your ideas a structure, provides a roadmap for your writing journey, and keeps you focused and organized. Incorporating AI into your outlining process can streamline this task and spark creative ideas.

AI can help generate a high-level structure of your book based on your initial ideas. Suppose you're writing a self-help book about overcoming procrastination. You can prompt your AI tool to generate a book outline by providing a brief description, like: "Create an outline for a self-help book titled 'Overcoming Procrastination: Step by Step Guide to Breaking Free from Procrastination for Good.'" Depending on your AI tool's capabilities, it might generate a detailed outline with chapter titles, subheadings, and even a short summary of each chapter.

You can then review this AI-generated outline, refine it, and customize it to match your vision for the book. Remember, the AI doesn't understand your unique vision or the specific message you want to convey. It's up to you to guide the AI and mold its output to fit your requirements.

Additionally, AI can assist you in structuring each chapter. For example, you can prompt the AI to generate a chapter outline for "Understanding Procrastination: The Science Behind It." The AI might come up with subheadings like "The Psychology of Procrastination," "How Procrastination Affects the Brain," and "Common Triggers of Procrastination."

Generating Chapter Ideas with AI

One of the most challenging parts of writing a book is coming up with compelling chapter ideas that flow together seamlessly. Here again, AI can be of assistance.

You can prompt your AI tool to generate a list of chapter ideas based on your book's theme. For instance, for a book on overcoming procrastination, your prompt could be: "Generate ten chapter ideas for a self-help book on overcoming procrastination." The AI might come up with chapter ideas like "The Mindset of a Procrastinator," "Procrastination and Self-esteem," "Strategies to Beat Procrastination," and "Maintaining Momentum: How to Avoid Falling Back into Procrastination."

Remember to review and refine these AI-generated ideas. Not all of them may fit into your book, or you may want to combine several ideas into a single chapter. Use these ideas as a starting point, a springboard to stimulate your creativity and develop your unique chapter ideas.

AI-Assisted Research for Your Book

Research is a crucial part of writing a book. Whether you're writing a historical novel, a business book, a cookbook, or a self-help book, you'll need to conduct thorough research to ensure your book is accurate, credible, and engaging.

AI can streamline your research process in several ways. There are AI tools that can summarize articles, scan through large volumes of data, and present you with the key insights. For instance, if you're writing a book on overcoming procrastination, you might need to read several scientific papers on procrastination. An AI summarization tool can provide you with a concise summary of these papers, saving you hours of reading time.

There are also AI tools that can generate a list of credible sources for your research based on your book's theme. You can prompt the AI tool with something like: "Generate a list of credible sources for researching the psychology of procrastination." The AI tool might then provide you with a list of academic papers, books, experts in the field, and relevant websites.

AI can also assist in fact-checking, ensuring that your book is accurate and trustworthy. There are AI fact-checking tools that can scan your book and flag any potential inaccuracies. For instance, if you've mentioned a specific study in your book, the AI tool can check if your description of the study matches the original source.

However, while AI can streamline your research process, remember that it's not infallible. Always double-check the AI's output and ensure that you're using reliable AI tools for your research.

Incorporating AI into your book writing process can

greatly enhance your productivity and creativity. Whether you're planning your book outline, generating chapter ideas, or conducting research, AI can assist you every step of the way. Remember, though, that AI is a tool, a powerful one, but it does not replace the creativity, critical thinking, and unique insights that you bring to your writing.

AI as a Creative Companion

AI can serve as a creative companion in your book writing journey, assisting you with brainstorming sessions, providing instant feedback, and even serving as an interactive writing prompt generator. For instance, if you're feeling stuck or experiencing writer's block, you can ask the AI for a writing prompt based on your book's theme to stimulate your creativity and get the words flowing again.

Additionally, advanced AI models can generate character sketches, plot suggestions, or setting descriptions. Suppose you're writing a science fiction novel and need a unique alien creature. You can prompt the AI with something like: "Describe a unique alien creature that lives on a planet with harsh, desert-like conditions." The AI might generate a vivid description, sparking your imagination and contributing to your world-building process.

However, remember that AI-generated content is just a starting point. It's up to you to refine these ideas, add depth and complexity, and infuse them with your unique voice and style.

AI and Editing

Editing is a crucial part of writing a book, and here, too, AI can lend a helping hand. There are several AI-powered editing tools that can analyze your book for grammar, punctuation, and spelling errors, inconsistent tense usage, passive voice, overly complex sentences, and even clichés. These tools can help polish your manuscript, making it ready for the next steps of publishing.

Additionally, there are AI tools that can provide stylistic suggestions, such as enhancing your vocabulary, varying your sentence structure, or improving the flow of your writing. Some tools can even analyze your writing style, provide feedback on readability, and suggest changes to match the reading level of your target audience.

Again, while these AI tools can be incredibly helpful, remember that they are not infallible. Always review the AI's suggestions and decide whether they enhance your manuscript or not. The final decision always lies with you.

AI in the Publishing Process

Once your manuscript is polished and ready to go, AI can assist in the publishing process as well. There are AI tools that can generate a compelling book blurb, help design your book cover, or determine the optimal price for your book based on market trends.

AI can also help with marketing your book. For instance, there are AI tools that can analyze market trends, identify your target audience, and suggest effective marketing strategies. Some tools can even create engaging social media posts, blog content, or email newsletters to promote your book.

In Conclusion

Incorporating AI into your book writing process can make the process smoother, more efficient, and even more enjoyable. From outlining to generating chapter ideas, conducting research, editing, and publishing, AI can serve as a powerful assistant, supplementing your skills and streamlining the process.

However, never forget that you are the heart and soul of your book. AI is merely a tool, a powerful one, but it's your creativity, your insights, your unique voice, and style that will make your book truly stand out. Embrace the assistance of AI, but don't lose your unique touch in the process and find a structure that speaks to what you want to achieve with your book.

CHAPTER 8

BUILDING CHARACTERS AND PLOT WITH AI

Using AI for Character Development

Crafting compelling characters is one of the most critical aspects of storytelling. Readers connect with characters, empathize with their struggles, and celebrate their victories. Characters drive the plot, and their motivations, personalities, and backstories make the story engaging and memorable. In this part of your writing journey, AI can assist you with character development.

AI writing tools can help generate character profiles based on various parameters. For instance, you can prompt the AI with something like: "Create a profile for a protagonist who is a 30-year-old detective with a sharp mind, a quirky sense of humor, and a troubled past." The AI could generate a detailed character profile, including the character's physical appearance, personality traits, backstory, habits, preferences, relationships, etc. This can serve as a starting point, which you can refine and develop further.

AI can also assist in developing character arcs. You can prompt the AI to suggest a character arc for your protagonist or any other character. For example, your prompt could be: "Suggest a character arc for a detective who starts as a cynical, lone wolf but needs to learn the value of trust and teamwork." The AI might provide a rough sketch of this character arc, outlining the character's initial state, the challenges they face, their evolution, and their state by the end of the story.

Remember that while AI can generate ideas and suggestions, it doesn't understand your characters as deeply as you do. AI doesn't comprehend human emotions, motivations, or complex character relationships. It's your job as the author to breathe life into these AI-generated profiles and arcs, to infuse them with depth, complexity, and authenticity.

AI-Assisted Plot Generation

A well-crafted plot is the backbone of any story. It's the series of events that propels your characters towards their goals, presents them with challenges, and brings about change and growth. Crafting a compelling plot can be a complex task, and here, too, AI can help.

AI writing tools can generate plot ideas based on your story's genre, theme, or characters. For example, you can prompt the AI with: "Generate a plot for a mystery novel set in a small coastal town with a detective protagonist." The AI might come up with a unique plot, involving a series of mysterious disappearances, a town full of secrets, and a race against time to solve the mystery.

AI can also assist in structuring your plot. You can prompt the AI to generate a plot structure based on various plot frameworks, like the three-act structure, the hero's journey, or the mystery plot structure. The AI can provide a rough sketch of your plot, outlining the inciting incident, the rising action, the climax, the falling action, and the resolution. This can serve as a roadmap for your writing, which you can customize and develop further.

Again, remember that while AI can generate plot ideas and structures, it doesn't understand your unique vision for your story. The AI doesn't comprehend the emotional depth, thematic nuances, or the symbolic meaning of your plot. As the author, it's your responsibility to take these AI-generated ideas and transform them into a compelling, engaging plot that resonates with your readers.

Experimenting with AI-
Generated Scenarios

One of the exciting aspects of AI writing tools is their ability to generate unexpected, out-of-the-box ideas. These AI-generated scenarios can stimulate your creativity, inspire new plot twists, or introduce unexpected character developments.

For instance, you can prompt the AI with something like: "Generate a surprising plot twist for a detective story involving a mysterious disappearance." The AI might suggest a plot twist involving an unexpected suspect, a hidden motive, or a shocking revelation about the detective's past. This can provide fresh inspiration, adding a new layer of intrigue to your story.

Or you can use AI to explore different scenarios for your characters. For example, you can ask the AI: "What would happen if my protagonist, the detective, suddenly lost her investigative abilities?" The AI might generate a scenario where the detective must rely on her overlooked interpersonal skills, introducing a new character dynamic, and pushing the detective's character development in a new direction.

Remember, these AI-generated scenarios are merely suggestions. They may not always align with your story's direction or your characters' personalities. However, they can stimulate your imagination, push you to think outside the box, and inspire fresh ideas. Always consider the AI's suggestions critically and choose the ones that enhance your story and resonate with your creative vision.

In conclusion, AI can be a valuable assistant in building your characters and crafting your plot. Whether you're developing character profiles, crafting plot structures, or experimenting with unexpected scenarios, AI can provide a steady stream of ideas and suggestions. However, always remember that you, the author, are the ultimate creative force behind your story. Use the AI as a tool, but never let it overshadow your unique creative voice and vision.

Going Deeper with AI-Generated Characters

As your story develops, so too will your characters. Their motivations will evolve, their personalities may change, and they may experience significant growth or transformation. With AI, you can explore these developmental arcs in a dynamic and stimulating way.

Consider prompting your AI tool with specific character changes you're considering, or even uncertainties you have about where your characters should go. For instance, you could input: "Show how my detective character might react if she found out her trusted partner was the mastermind behind the crimes she's investigating." AI can help envisage these scenarios, providing you with a fresh perspective on your characters and their potential paths.

Don't forget that an AI's suggestions are not prescriptive but rather possibilities worth exploring. The AI doesn't understand the depth of human emotion or the complexity of character evolution, but it can generate ideas that you, the writer, can take and mold into something deeply human and profoundly engaging.

Exploring Multiple Plot Directions with AI

Another way AI can enhance your writing process is by enabling you to explore multiple plot directions quickly and efficiently. There are moments in the writing process where you may feel stuck or uncertain about where your plot should head next. AI can help by generating several different plot progressions based on your current story.

For instance, you might be unsure whether your detective should discover a significant clue in the next chapter, or whether she should face a setback that complicates her investigation. You could prompt your AI tool with these different scenarios and see how they might unfold, helping you decide which direction feels more engaging and truer to your story.

AI and Genre Conventions

AI can also help you adhere to or break away from genre conventions. If you're writing a mystery novel, there are certain tropes and conventions that readers may expect, and others you might want to avoid keeping your story fresh and unpredictable. AI can help generate plot points or character arcs that either adhere to these conventions or subvert them in surprising ways.

For instance, you can prompt your AI with a genre-specific request like: "Generate a plot twist for a detective novel that subverts the typical conventions of the mystery genre." This way, you can ensure your story feels unique and avoids clichés, while still satisfying the expectations of your target audience.

Using AI for World-Building

Beyond characters and plots, another essential component of any good story is the setting or the world in which it unfolds. Whether it's a quaint small town, a bustling metropolis, or a distant alien planet, the setting can add depth and richness to your story. It can create a sense of atmosphere, influence the plot and character development, and serve as a vehicle for themes and symbolism.

AI can assist you with world-building in several ways. For example, you can prompt the AI to generate descriptions of your settings based on certain parameters. If you're writing a detective novel set in a small coastal town, you could prompt the AI with: "Describe a small coastal town in the Pacific Northwest in the late fall." The AI might generate a vivid, atmospheric description of the town, capturing its charm, the beauty of the changing seasons, the scent of the sea, and the quiet melancholy that envelopes the town.

Similarly, AI can assist in creating the social, political, or cultural context of your world. You can prompt the AI to generate a history for your town, a political conflict that's brewing, a local legend that haunts the town folk, or a cultural festival that's being celebrated. This can add layers of depth and realism to your world, making it feel lived-in and authentic.

Again, remember to use the AI-generated content as a starting point and infuse it with your creative vision. AI doesn't understand the atmospheric nuances, the symbolic potential, or the thematic significance of your settings. As the author, it's your responsibility to bring your world to life and make it resonate with your readers.

AI for Continuity and Consistency

Another area where AI can be particularly useful is ensuring continuity and consistency in your story. As your plot becomes more complex and your characters more developed, keeping track of all the details can become challenging. Here, AI can serve as a helpful tool.

You can prompt the AI to recall and summarize plot points or character details. For example, you can ask the AI: "Summarize the key events in my story so far," or "Describe my protagonist's character development until now." The AI can provide a quick recap, helping you ensure consistency in your narrative.

However, it's important to note that AI's ability to recall and summarize is based on the information you've provided it with. The AI doesn't have an understanding or memory of your story beyond that. Hence, always cross-check the AI's recaps with your notes or drafts.

Summary

AI can be an exciting tool for character and plot development, offering a myriad of possibilities to explore. While it doesn't possess the deep understanding of human emotion and character complexity that you as a writer do, it can serve as a brainstorming partner, idea generator, and creative stimulant.

AI can aid you in shaping dynamic, compelling characters, creating engaging and surprising plots, and ensuring your story stays fresh and appealing. Remember, though, to maintain your unique authorial voice and creative control. AI is an assistant in the creative process, but you are the author – the heart and soul of your story.

CHAPTER 9

EDITING YOUR BOOK WITH AI

Once you've finished writing your book, the next crucial step is editing and polishing your manuscript. This is where you refine your story, correct grammar, and syntax errors, enhance the narrative flow, and elevate your prose. AI tools can prove invaluable during this process, not only as grammar and style checkers but also as aids in enhancing the narrative flow and refining the prose. In this chapter, we will explore how to make the best use of AI during the editing and polishing phase of your book.

AI Tools for Grammar and Style Checks

The first line of editing typically involves checking for grammatical errors, awkward phrasing, redundancies, and inconsistencies in style. While human editors are excellent at this, they can sometimes overlook minor errors or typos. This is where AI-based grammar and style checkers come in. These tools are designed to spot a wide range of potential issues in your text, from basic spelling and grammar mistakes to more nuanced issues like passive voice, wordiness, or tone inconsistencies.

Grammarly, for instance, is an AI-based tool that analyzes your text for grammatical and stylistic errors and provides real-time suggestions for improvement. It can detect spelling mistakes, punctuation errors, incorrect word usage, and even more complex grammatical issues like dangling modifiers or incorrect verb tenses. It also provides style recommendations, such as removing unnecessary words, shifting from passive to active voice, or making your sentences more concise.

Another popular AI-based tool is ProWritingAid, which offers comprehensive feedback on your writing style and technique, in addition to basic grammar and spelling checks. It can analyze your manuscript for elements like readability, sentence variation, overused words, transitions, and more, helping you improve the overall quality and flow of your writing.

Remember, though, while these AI tools can be incredibly useful for catching errors and polishing your style, they're not infallible. Always review the suggestions critically and consider whether they align with your voice and the intent of your sentence. Additionally, certain aspects of writing, such as tone, nuance, or creative style, are still best judged by a human eye.

Enhancing Narrative Flow with AI

Beyond grammar and style checks, another critical aspect of editing is ensuring a smooth and coherent narrative flow. This involves checking that your story progresses logically, that there are smooth transitions between scenes or chapters, and that your prose creates a rhythmic, engaging reading experience.

AI tools can assist with this process in a variety of ways. For instance, some AI-based editing tools can analyze your manuscript for structural issues, such as disjointed narratives, pacing problems, or lack of variety in sentence lengths. Tools like AutoCrit or Fictionary can provide detailed structural analysis of your manuscript, pointing out potential issues and areas for improvement.

Another way to use AI to enhance narrative flow is by generating transition sentences or paragraphs. If you're struggling with a transition between two scenes or chapters, you can prompt your AI writing tool to generate a transition based on the preceding and following content. This can help you maintain a smooth narrative progression and keep your readers engaged.

Additionally, AI can assist in refining your prose for a better rhythm and flow. If you feel a particular paragraph is choppy or lacks rhythm, you can input it into your AI writing tool and ask for a smoother version. The AI can rearrange the sentences, alter the sentence lengths, or suggest different phrasing to create a more rhythmic, flowing prose.

Reviewing and Refining
AI Suggestions

While AI can provide valuable suggestions and insights during the editing process, it's essential to review and refine these suggestions critically. AI doesn't understand the deeper nuances of your story, the subtleties of your characters, or the specific rhythm and voice of your prose. It can only analyze based on patterns, algorithms, and pre-fed data.

When reviewing AI suggestions, always consider whether they align with your story's intent, your characters' voices, and your unique writing style. If a suggested change alters the meaning of a sentence, dilutes a character's voice, or disrupts the rhythm of your prose, feel free to disregard it.

Also, remember to use AI tools as aids, not substitutes for human editing. While AI tools can catch a lot of errors and provide useful suggestions, a human editor's insight, expertise, and nuanced understanding of language are invaluable. A professional editor can catch inconsistencies in plot or character development, point out potential plot holes, provide feedback on the pacing and tension in your story, and offer suggestions to enhance the emotional impact of your writing. These are aspects that AI, at least currently, can't fully grasp or assist with.

Advanced AI Editing Tools

With advancements in AI technology, several AI tools have emerged that take editing and proofreading a step further. These tools, often trained on large datasets of professionally published literature, can analyze your text for more complex issues like inconsistent character behavior, plot inconsistencies, and problems with the structure or pacing of your story.

One such tool is Marlowe, an AI writing assistant developed by OpenAI, which goes beyond grammar and style checks. It can provide feedback on the plot and character development, point out passages that might confuse readers, and suggest improvements to the pacing and structure of your story.

Another tool, called Hemingway, is particularly useful for making your writing more concise and clearer to your reader. It highlights sentences that are hard to read, suggests simpler alternatives for complex words or phrases, and points out instances where you've used passive voice or too many adverbs.

Remember, though, that while these tools can provide valuable insights and suggestions, they're not infallible. Always review the suggestions critically and consider whether they align with your voice and the intent of your sentence. Certain aspects of writing, such as tone, nuance, or creative style, are still best judged by a human eye.

Striking a Balance

While AI can be an excellent tool for self-editing and proofreading, it is not meant to replace professional human editing. After you've gone through your manuscript with the help of AI tools, it's highly recommended to have a human editor go through it as well.

A professional editor can provide a level of feedback and understanding that AI, at least currently, can't fully replicate. They bring their unique insight, experience, and subjective judgment to the editing process, catching things an AI might miss and adding a personal touch that AI lacks.

Moreover, human editors understand your audience and the market trends in a way AI cannot. They can help shape your manuscript in a way that not only polishes the writing but also makes it more appealing to your target readers and more marketable to publishers.

Using AI tools before handing your manuscript over to a human editor can make the process more efficient, though. The AI can take care of the more mundane tasks of editing—correcting spelling and grammar mistakes, flagging passive voice and adverbs, checking for repetition—and free up the human editor to focus on the more complex and nuanced aspects of editing.

In conclusion, when it comes to editing and polishing your book, AI is best used in combination with professional human editing. Let AI take care of the initial rounds of proofreading and basic editing, and then bring in a human editor for the final rounds of editing and polishing. This way, you can ensure your manuscript is as polished and professionally presented as possible.

CHAPTER 10

PUBLISHING AND PROMOTING YOUR BOOK

The final milestone in your journey as an author is publishing your book. Publishing isn't just about printing your manuscript; it's a multifaceted process that involves choosing a publishing path, pitching your book, working with editors and cover designers, marketing, and promotion, and much more. Thankfully, AI can assist you in these tasks as well, making the publishing process more streamlined and efficient. In this chapter, we'll explore the publishing choices you have, and how AI can assist in book marketing and promotion.

Traditional Publishing vs. Self-Publishing: What to Choose?

Before we delve into how AI can assist in publishing, let's first understand the two primary publishing paths available to you: traditional publishing and self-publishing.

Traditional publishing involves submitting your manuscript to established publishing houses or literary agents. If your manuscript is accepted, the publishing house takes over the tasks of editing, designing, printing, distributing, and marketing your book. In return, you receive an advance and royalties on book sales. Traditional publishing can lend credibility and provide extensive reach, but it's often a long, competitive process with less control over the final product.

On the other hand, self-publishing gives you complete control over the entire process. You're responsible for editing, designing, printing, distributing, and marketing your book. While self-publishing requires more work and upfront investment, it offers higher royalties, complete creative control, and a quicker path to publication.

The choice between traditional and self-publishing depends on your goals, resources, and how much control you wish to have over the process. Do your research, understand the pros and cons of each option, and choose the one that aligns best with your needs.

How AI Can Help in Book
Marketing and Promotion

Once you've decided on your publishing path and your book is ready to be shared with the world, the next step is marketing and promotion. This is where AI can be a powerful ally. It can help in various aspects of marketing, such as market research, audience segmentation, content creation, and data analysis.

Market Research: AI tools can help identify trends in the book market, popular genres, themes, or tropes, and understand what readers are currently interested in. Tools like K-lytics or Publisher Rocket can provide valuable market insights, helping you position your book effectively.

Audience Segmentation: AI can also help in segmenting your audience, i.e., identifying the specific groups of people who would be interested in your book. AI can analyze data from various sources, like social media, online forums, and book review sites, to identify patterns and trends that can help you understand your target audience better.

Content Creation: AI can assist in creating promotional content for your book. Whether it's writing compelling book descriptions, crafting social media posts, or generating ideas for blog posts, AI can help. You can use an AI writing tool like Jarvis (also known as Conversion.ai) to generate creative, engaging content for your marketing campaigns.

Data Analysis: AI can analyze the performance of your marketing campaigns, providing insights into what's working and what's not. This can help you optimize your strategies and ensure your marketing efforts are effective.

AI in Generating a Catchy Book Title and Effective Blurb

Creating a catchy and appealing book title can be a daunting task, but AI can help here too. Certain AI tools can generate a list of potential titles based on the themes, genre, and style of your book. Remember, a great book title can make a substantial difference in attracting potential readers and setting the right expectations for what they will find inside.

Similarly, writing an effective book blurb, the short description that goes on the back cover of your book, is critical to hook potential readers. AI writing assistants can help you craft a compelling blurb by suggesting impactful sentences, advising on length and structure, or even generating entire drafts based on your book's content.

AI and Book Cover Design

The adage "Don't judge a book by its cover" doesn't really apply in the publishing world. A book's cover is its primary marketing tool, an invitation for readers to explore the story within. Thankfully, AI can assist here too.

Some AI tools can generate book cover designs based on the book's title, genre, and themes. These tools analyze successful book covers in your genre and use that data to generate designs that are likely to appeal to your target readership. Remember, though, that while these AI-generated designs can be a great starting point, you might still need a professional designer's touch to ensure a high-quality, polished finished product.

AI and Building Your Author Platform

Building an author platform, your social media presence, and a website is critical for both self-publishing and traditionally publishing authors. It's a way to connect with your readers, build a community, and market your book.

AI can assist in managing and growing your author platform. For example, AI tools can schedule social media posts at optimal times, suggest content based on trending topics, and even automate responses to common comments or messages. AI can also analyze your website and social media performance, providing insights to optimize your online presence.

AI in Email Marketing

For many authors, email marketing is a key strategy. AI can help you segment your email list, personalize your emails, optimize email subject lines, and analyze the performance of your email campaigns.

For instance, AI tools can analyze your subscribers' behavior to identify what kind of content engages them the most, what time they're most likely to read your emails, and what subject lines get the highest open rates. This data can help you craft more effective, targeted email campaigns.

To summarize, AI offers numerous ways to assist with marketing and promoting your book. From generating a catchy book title and blurb to designing your book cover, building your author platform, and optimizing your email marketing, AI can make the process more efficient and effective.

Remember, while AI can provide valuable assistance in marketing and promoting your book, it doesn't replace human effort and creativity. Always bring your personal touch to your marketing campaigns, interact genuinely with your audience, and use AI as a tool to assist you, not as a replacement for your efforts.

CHAPTER 11

ETHICS OF AI IN WRITING

Artificial intelligence, while a powerful tool in writing, isn't devoid of ethical considerations. The advent of AI in writing has sparked debates about ownership, copyright issues, and ethical boundaries. It is vital to navigate these waters carefully, understanding the potential implications and acting responsibly. In this chapter, we'll explore the ethics of AI in writing, focusing on ownership and copyright issues, and broader ethical considerations.

Ownership and Copyright Issues

When you use an AI tool to write, who owns the final product? If an AI generates a piece of writing, who holds the copyright to that work? These are complex questions that the current legal framework struggles to answer.

Traditionally, copyright law assigns ownership to the 'creator' of a work. But when an AI generates a text, it's challenging to identify who the creator is. Is it the AI that produced the text? Or the programmer who created the AI? Or is it you, who input the prompts and curated the output?

Current copyright law varies from country to country, and it's evolving to accommodate these new challenges. In general, though, it tends to lean towards the person who made a creative contribution. If you input the prompts and guide the AI, you are likely to be considered the creator, holding the copyright to the final output.

However, this is a grey area and interpretation may vary. Therefore, it's essential to check with legal counsel or refer to the specific terms and conditions of your AI tool to understand how they handle copyright issues.

Ethical Considerations When Using AI in Writing

Beyond ownership and copyright, there are broader ethical issues to consider when using AI in writing.

Authenticity: If you're using AI to assist in your writing, it's essential to be transparent about it. Misleading readers into believing a human entirely wrote a piece when it's AI-generated can be considered unethical. A balance must be struck where AI aids the writing process without compromising the authenticity of the work.

Quality and Originality: While AI can generate text based on existing data, it might not always be able to match the originality and creative quality of human writing. Overreliance on AI could lead to generic or derivative content. Ethically, it's crucial to use AI as a tool to enhance original, creative writing, rather than a shortcut to replace it.

Privacy: AI writing tools learn from massive datasets, often including user-input data. While reputable AI developers anonymize and aggregate data, the privacy concern is real. Ethically, it's essential to use AI tools that respect user privacy and abide by data protection laws.

Bias: AI models learn from data, and if the data contains bias, the AI could perpetuate that bias in its output. This is a significant ethical concern when using AI in writing. It's important to critically evaluate the AI's output, correct any biases, and commit to using AI in a way that promotes fairness and diversity.

Avoiding Plagiarism with AI

A particularly noteworthy ethical concern when using AI in writing is the risk of unintentional plagiarism. As AI language models are trained on vast amounts of data from the internet, they don't distinguish between common knowledge and proprietary information. If the AI model generates content that mirrors another author's work too closely, it could lead to plagiarism allegations.

To mitigate this risk, consider using plagiarism detection tools on AI-generated content to ensure originality. Also, constantly iterate on the AI output, adding your unique perspective and voice. Always strive for originality and creativity, using AI as an aid, not a replacement for your unique voice.

Ethical Use of AI in Journalism

AI has found its way into journalism as well, where it's used to write reports, particularly in data-heavy areas like sports or financial news. While this can increase efficiency and speed, ethical considerations arise. For instance, is it ethical to replace human reporters with AI? What about the potential loss of nuance and depth in reporting?

When using AI in journalism, it's essential to maintain transparency and distinguish between human-written and AI-written articles. Moreover, even though AI can write basic reports, human journalists are still needed for in-depth analysis, interviews, and investigative journalism. The goal should be to use AI to free up human journalists for more complex tasks, not replace them entirely.

AI and Creative Writing

In creative writing, AI can be a co-creator, providing inspiration and generating initial drafts. But here, too, ethical considerations come into play. How much AI-generated content can you use before your work loses its human touch? To what extent can you claim a novel written with substantial AI assistance as your own?

While there are no hard and fast rules, the principle of transparency applies here as well. Acknowledge the role of AI in your writing process. In addition, ensure that your work maintains a unique voice and perspective – the AI is a tool, but you're the author.

AI's Impact on Jobs in Writing

AI has the potential to automate some writing tasks, leading to concerns about job displacement. The ethical responsibility here falls not just on individual writers, but also on businesses, industries, and regulators.

While it's true that AI might automate some tasks, it's unlikely to replace human writers entirely. Writing is not just about stringing words together; it's about connecting with the reader, understanding cultural nuances, and creating an emotional impact – things that AI cannot replicate.

Moreover, the advent of AI also creates new job opportunities, such as training AI models, overseeing AI outputs, and roles that we can't even envision yet. As with any technological advancement, the key is to adapt, learn new skills, and find ways to work with technology, not against it.

In conclusion, ethical considerations are paramount when using AI in writing. Respect for copyright and ownership, maintaining authenticity, striving for originality, upholding privacy, correcting bias, avoiding plagiarism, and considering the broader impact on jobs are all crucial. While navigating this new territory can be challenging, it's also an opportunity to redefine writing ethics in the age of AI.

CHAPTER 12

THE FUTURE OF AI
IN WRITING

The realm of AI in writing is continually evolving. Each day, new developments push the boundaries of what AI can achieve, reshaping our understanding of creativity and authorship. In this penultimate chapter, we'll look at some of the latest advancements in AI writing and what potential future developments might bring.

Latest Developments in AI and Writing

AI language models have made significant strides in recent years. Advances in machine learning algorithms and computational power have led to AI models like GPT-4, which can generate remarkably coherent and contextually relevant text.

Today, AI can generate news articles, blog posts, poems, short stories, and even entire novels. It can mimic different writing styles, adapt to various genres, and provide instant feedback on grammar, style, and tone. Tools like OpenAI's ChatGPT have shown impressive abilities to understand context, recall relevant information, and maintain long conversations, transforming the landscape of customer service, content generation, and more.

Another promising development is the advent of AI translation tools that are rapidly becoming more sophisticated. AI can now translate text between multiple languages with remarkable accuracy, considering context, cultural nuances, and idiomatic expressions. This could revolutionize the publishing industry, allowing books to reach a global audience faster and more efficiently.

AI has also found a place in the educational sector, providing personalized feedback to students, suggesting improvements, and even generating questions and exercises based on a given text. This can augment the learning experience, providing students with instant, customized support.

Potential Future Advances

While it's impossible to predict the future with certainty, we can make educated guesses based on current trends in the field. Here are some potential future advances in AI writing:

1. Improved Contextual Understanding and Creativity: Future AI models will likely have a deeper understanding of context, being able to maintain long, coherent narratives over extended pieces of text. They might also become more creative, generating more original ideas, plot twists in storytelling, and innovative problem-solving strategies.

2. Personalized AI Writing Assistants: We could see AI writing assistants becoming highly personalized, adapting to an individual's writing style, preferences, and goals. These AI models might be able to learn from your previous writings, suggest ideas you're likely to be interested in, and provide feedback tailored to your unique voice.

3. Real-Time Collaboration: AI might facilitate real-time collaboration between multiple authors, suggesting ideas, mediating conflicts, and ensuring a consistent writing style across the collaborative piece. It could also allow for real-time translation, enabling collaboration between authors who don't speak the same language.

4. Multimedia Content Generation: AI might expand beyond text, generating multimedia content. Imagine an AI that could write a screenplay and then create an animated video to go along with it. This could open new horizons in filmmaking, advertising, and content creation.

5. Ethics and Regulations: As AI writing becomes more prevalent, we'll likely see an evolution in ethics and regulations. Copyright laws might need to be revised to account for AI-generated content, and ethical guidelines might be established to ensure the responsible use of AI in writing.

Deep Dive into Future Advances

Let's delve deeper into the potential future advances we previously outlined, exploring them in more detail and discussing their possible implications.

Improved Contextual
Understanding and Creativity

The future of AI writing lies in the development of models that have a more sophisticated understanding of context. In terms of creativity, AI could learn to invent original characters, come up with unexpected plot twists, and perhaps even create new genres. To illustrate this, we could see AI becoming a central tool in creating interactive narratives, such as video games or immersive VR experiences. With the ability to generate narratives in real-time based on user actions, AI might play a significant role in creating truly immersive, dynamic storytelling experiences.

Personalized AI Writing Assistants

Personalized AI writing assistants could transform the writing process. Imagine a tool that not only corrects your grammar but also understands your unique voice and style. This AI could provide personalized feedback, suggest ways to enhance your narrative, and even predict what you're trying to write. By learning from your past works, the AI would gain a deeper understanding of your writing style and could provide insights that you might not have considered. In the world of book writing, this could make the writing process more efficient and enjoyable, allowing authors to focus more on creativity and less on technicalities.

Real-Time Collaboration

The future may hold advanced collaborative tools powered by AI. These tools could facilitate real-time collaborations between authors, irrespective of their geographical locations. AI could suggest ideas to bridge differing writing styles, ensure consistency across the collaborative piece, and even allow for real-time translation, opening the door for global collaborations. For publishing houses and content creation teams, this could mean seamless integration of efforts and ideas, leading to more cohesive and high-quality outputs.

Multimedia Content Generation

As AI evolves, it may expand into the realm of multimedia content creation. For instance, AI could create animations or virtual reality experiences based on the narratives it generates. Imagine writing a screenplay and having an AI instantly create an animated video to visualize it. This integration of text and visual media could revolutionize fields like filmmaking, advertising, and education, making them more accessible and versatile.

Ethics and Regulations

As AI becomes an integral part of the writing landscape, we will need robust ethics and regulations to ensure its responsible use. Issues of data privacy, copyright infringement, and job displacement need to be thoughtfully considered. As AI-generated content becomes increasingly indistinguishable from human-written content, we will need guidelines to maintain transparency and accountability. The laws surrounding copyright and ownership might need revisions to accommodate AI's role in content generation.

AI and Accessibility

Another potential future direction is the role of AI in making writing more accessible. AI could be used to provide real-time writing assistance for people with dyslexia or similar conditions, or to convert complex text into a simpler version for people with cognitive impairments or those learning a new language. It could also be used to instantly convert written content into an audio format for the visually impaired. The possibilities for how AI can make writing more accessible are vast and exciting.

While these potential advances are exciting, they also come with challenges. Issues such as data privacy, job displacement, and the risk of creating AI content that is indistinguishable from human writing are all areas of concern that will need to be addressed. As we embrace these advancements, we must also navigate the associated ethical and societal challenges responsibly. The goal should always be to use AI to make writing more accessible, efficient, and fun for everyone.

In conclusion, the future of AI in writing is teeming with possibilities. However, these advancements will also bring challenges. It will be our collective responsibility to navigate these challenges wisely, ensuring that the future of AI in writing is shaped in a way that benefits all of society.

CHAPTER 13

FINAL THOUGHTS

Reflecting on Our Path

We've reached the closing pages of this book, a moment that calls for reflection on the diverse terrain we've traversed together. We embarked on a formidable expedition—across the fundamentals of good writing to the cutting-edge technology of artificial intelligence.

Our point of departure was the bedrock of good writing. We examined why robust writing skills are indispensable and their widespread influence across various fields and professions. We also revisited the heart of storytelling, its diverse forms, and styles. A journey through the exciting spectrum of genres available to us as writers and the unique writing styles that lend our work distinctive voice and character added a broader perspective.

After mastering our understanding of writing, we ventured into the intriguing world of artificial intelligence. We unpacked the complex concept of AI, looking into its multifaceted types and fascinating history in writing. Together, we scrutinized the myriad benefits AI brings to writing, along with its constraints, thus setting a realistic perspective on the capabilities of AI as a tool for writers.

Switching to a narrower lens, we turned our focus on AI

language models. The intricacies of natural language processing were decoded, laying the groundwork for these models, and providing an understanding of their functioning. This knowledge allowed us to fully appreciate their potential and how to effectively harness them in our writing endeavors.

With a solid understanding of AI, we transitioned to the practical aspect: starting to write with AI. We delved into how to select appropriate AI writing tools, establish an AI writing environment, and familiarize ourselves with the basic operations. We discovered the importance of guiding AI through effective prompts and explored strategies for harmonizing human creativity with AI assistance in a symbiotic writing process.

As we delved deeper, we witnessed the transformative power of AI in structuring our books. AI's potential in aiding the creation of book outlines, generating chapter ideas, and conducting research was a revelation.

Building characters and developing plots with AI emerged as one of the most stimulating phases of our exploration. We experienced firsthand the potential of AI in character development, plot generation, and creative scenario crafting. We realized the power of AI as a catalyst, sparking our imagination and pushing creative boundaries.

In the realm of editing and refining our books, we discovered AI's immense contributions. We explored AI's potential in improving grammar, enhancing style, and ensuring a seamless narrative flow. We learned to scrutinize and refine the AI's suggestions, ensuring our creative vision was never compromised.

In the realm of publishing, we weighed traditional publishing against self-publishing and considered which path may best suit our needs. We also examined how AI can revolutionize book marketing and promotion, opening unprecedented opportunities for reaching our readers.

Lastly, we addressed the more nuanced aspects of using AI in writing: the ethical considerations and copyright issues. It became evident how vital it is to tread this ground with care, maintaining the integrity of our work and our profession.

Embrace Learning and Innovation

As AI continues to evolve, its integration with writing will inevitably deepen and diversify. This evolution underscores the importance of lifelong learning and an openness to experimentation. Keep your curiosity alive, and let creativity be your guiding force. Welcome the unknown, try out new AI tools, test different strategies, and view mistakes as steppingstones to greater understanding and improvement.

The interaction between AI and human creativity is a dynamic one. As you train the AI and guide it in your writing, you also gain insights from it. This reciprocal learning not only enhances your understanding of AI but also expands your creative potential.

While embracing this exciting territory, it's crucial to maintain an ethical compass. As AI continues to blur the lines between human and machine-generated content, responsibly navigating these waters is paramount.

As you stand on the precipice of your exploration into AI-assisted writing, remember that this is just the beginning. A world of possibilities brimming with potential for heightened creativity, productivity, and enjoyment in your writing lies ahead. Here's to a future where AI and human creativity harmoniously coexist! Happy writing!

About the Author

James Brady is a data analyst with advanced degrees and training in mathematics and statistics. He has also studied neural networks and basic Ai systems through the MIT certificate program. He is physically disabled and has been using technology to assist him from a young age. James wants everyone to appreciate how the latest tools will change our everyday lives in new and exciting ways.

Acknowledgments

I would like to thank my family and friends for their encouragement. I also must give credit to the many educators who over the years have supported my interest in mathematics and science. Without a lifelong fascination with technology and its advancement this book would not have been possible.

Dive into the era of AI-enhanced creativity with 'Becoming an AI Author.' This detailed guidebook demystifies the integration of AI into the writing process, walking you through each step from conception to publication, enabling you to harness the power of AI while maintaining your unique creative voice.

UNTITLED

www.ingramcontent.com/pod-product-compliance
Lightning Source LLC
La Vergne TN
LVHW051656050326
832903LV00032B/3846